NICE
LITTLE TOWN
CHRISTMAS

Author

TANYA BOGEMA (STOLOVA)

ADULT COLORING BOOK

MW00934444

Hi! My name is Tatiana and I'm painter :)
Thank you so much that you are choosing my books in spite of many other books present on market. I really appreciate this.
Every time I start new project I think about how to make my book more interesting. And I can't do this without you. To do that I need to have your feedbacks. Communication with you is very very important for creation process. With your feedbacks you give me new ideas and inspiration for new books that become better and more interesting.
Sincerely yours, Tatiana.

Our group in facebook:
https://www.facebook.com/groups/1280996941971412/
Please, look at other books of author on page:
http://amazon.com/author/bogemasky

Nice Little Town Christmas - Adult Coloring Book

Copyright © 2017 Tatiana Bogema (Stolova)

ISBN-13: 978-1976414657
ISBN-10: 1976414652

THIS BOOK BELONGS TO

ILLUSTRATIONS
FROM
OTHER
MY
BOOKS

Halloween

CUTE GIRLS

NICE
LITTLE
TOWN
2

MAGIC
MASK

GREAT
LIONS

STEAMPUNK

STEAMPUNK
VOL 2

AWESOME
ANIMALS

Made in the USA
Coppell, TX
16 November 2019